BEETHOVEN

THE FIRST BOOK FOR PIANISTS

D0841762

EDITED BY WILLARD A. PALMER

CONTENTS

K. WoO refers to Kinsky, *Work without opus number.* The number following this designation refers to the number in Kinsky's *Thematisch-Bibliographisches Verzeichnis aller vollendeten Werke Ludwig van Beethovens* (List of all completed works of Ludwig van Beethoven). George Kinsky, a German musicologist, catalogued all of Beethoven's works. He assigned numbers where Beethoven did not write in an opus number. Kinsky's study gives us a chronological listing of all of Beethoven's compositions.

Second Edition

Copyright © MMI by Alfred Publishing Co., Inc.
All rights reserved. Printed in USA.
ISBN 0-7390-0776-9 (Book)
ISBN 0-7390-2235-0 (Book & CD)

Cover art: Ludwig van Beethoven *(1770–1827)*
by Karl Stieler (1781–1858)
Oil on canvas, 1819
Beethoven House, Bonn, Germany
Erich Lessing/Art Resource, NY

The selections included in this book are taken from *Beethoven—An Introduction to His Piano Works* (#607). For students and teachers who prefer an expanded introductory section and additional selections in a 64-page book, the publisher recommends the Beethoven introduction listed above.

Écossaise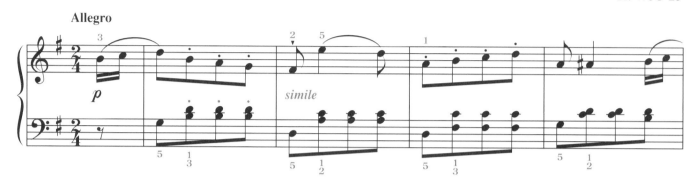

K. WoO 23

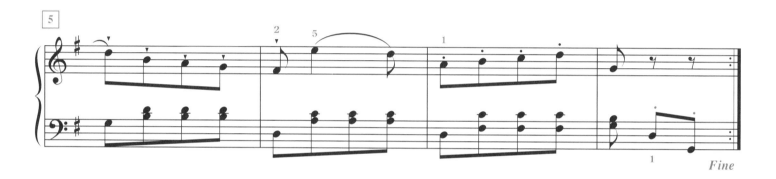

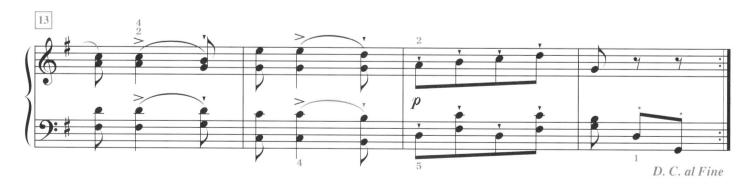

D. C. al Fine

ⓐ *Écossaise*, pronounced "ay-ko-sez," is a French word meaning "Scotch." The dance for which the music was composed does not have a Scottish origin, however. The Écossaise was a popular dance in ²₄ time, usually used for beginning and ending an evening of dancing. Chopin and Schubert also wrote Écossaises, and they are commonly subtitled "Scotch Dances."

Country Dance

K. WoO 15, No. 1

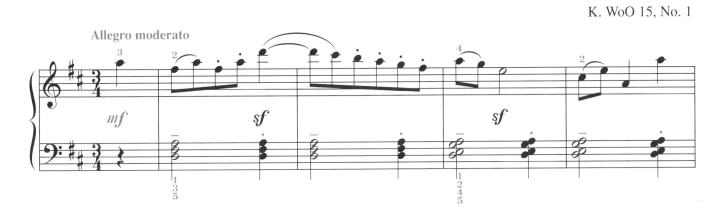

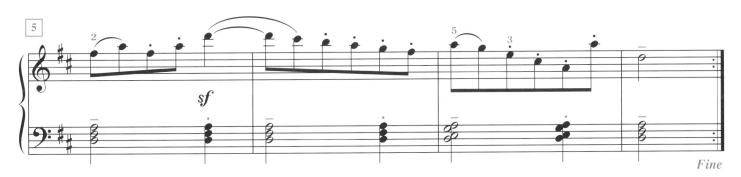

Country Dance

K. WoO 15, No. 2

Country Dance

K. WoO 11, No. 2

Lustig, Traurig

(Joyful, Sorrowful)

Lustig (Joyful)

K. WoO 54

il Fine

Menuet in C

K. WoO 10, No. 1

Moderato

Fine

TRIO

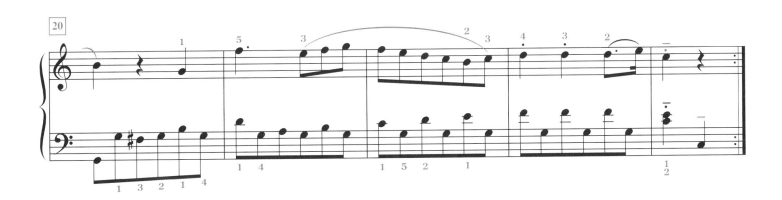

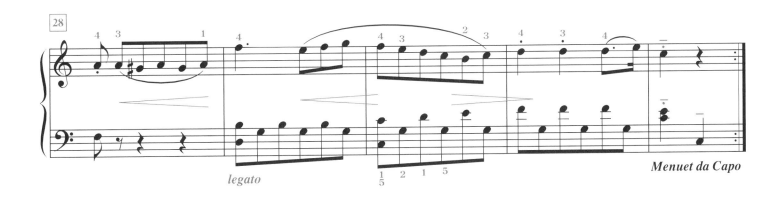

Menuet da Capo

Menuet in G

K. WoO 10, No. 2

ⓐ The following slurring, found in almost all modern editions, is not Beethoven's:

TRIO

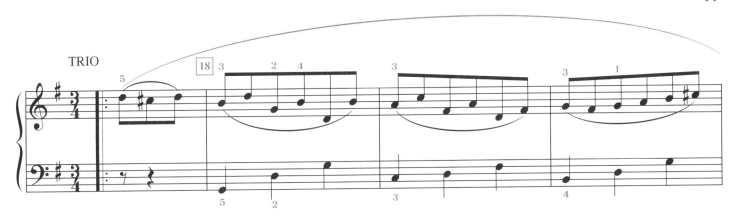

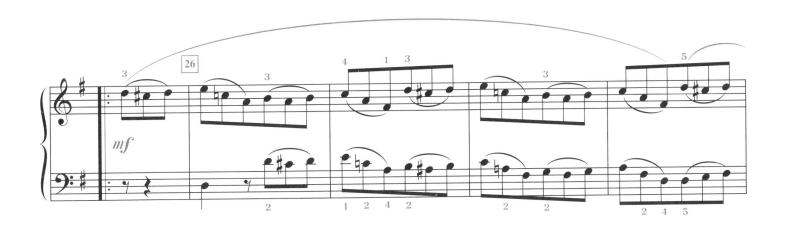

Menuet da Capo

Menuet in D

K. WoO 10, No. 5

Moderato e maestoso

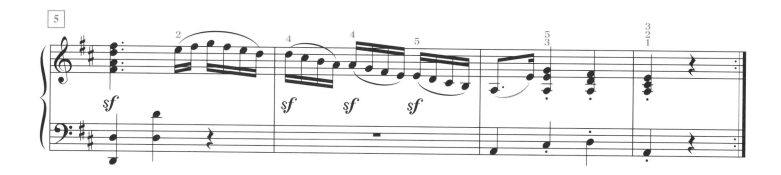

Fine

13

Menuet da Capo

Sonatina in G

ⓐ This appoggiatura may also be played thus:

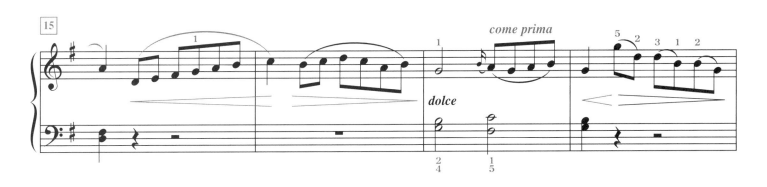

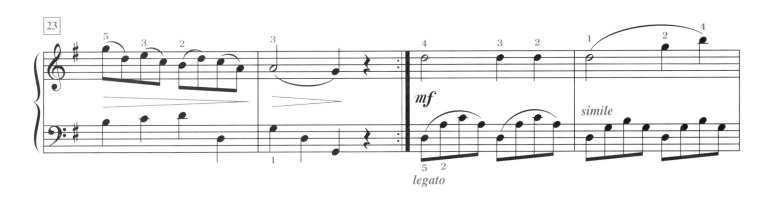

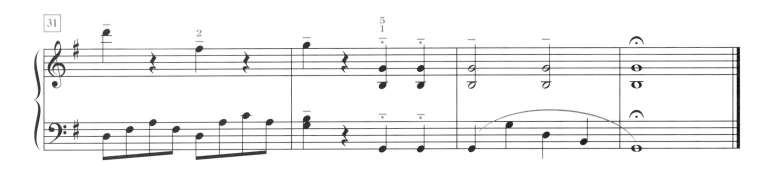

Sonata in G

(2nd movement)

Op. 49, No. 2

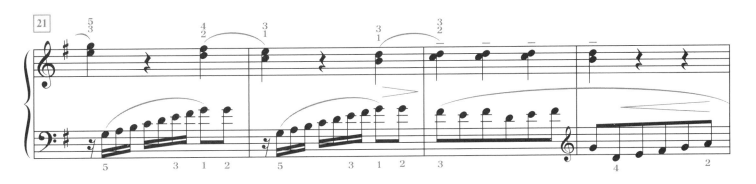

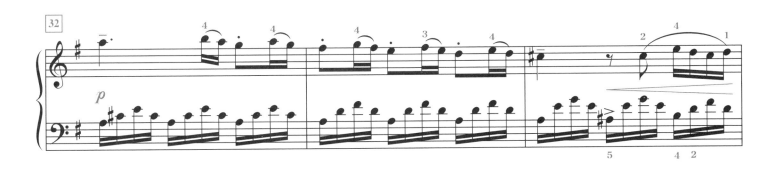

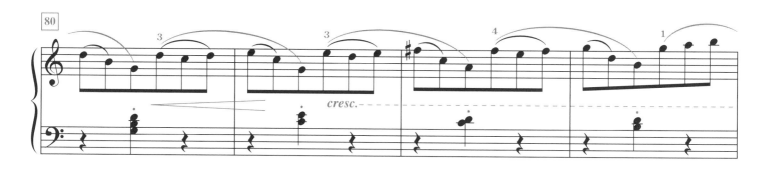

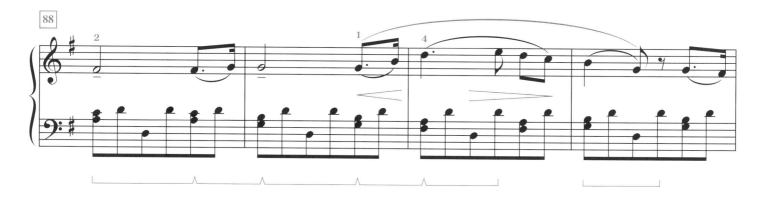

Ludwig van Beethoven (1770–1827)
Portrait by Carl Jäger

About the Music

All of the pieces in this book are in their original form, unsimplified. They have been thoroughly researched from the original autograph manuscripts and/or the earliest editions.

All the notes, slurs, dynamic signs, etc., in dark print are from the original sources. The indications in light gray print are editorial suggestions based on careful study of the performance practices of Beethoven's day.

ORNAMENTATION

The only ornaments that appear in this book are the single and double *appoggiatura:* ♪ ♫

All appoggiaturas in Beethoven's music are played *on the beat* and take their value from the following large note. Even the so-called "grace note" with a cross-stroke, which is found in some other editions, should be played *on the beat.* This is simply an old way of writing a sixteenth note, and it is used to indicate a *short appoggiatura.*

STACCATO INDICATIONS

Beethoven made a clear distinction between three types of staccato indications:

- THE WEDGE

This sign means that the note should be released instantly. In Beethoven's music it does not imply any special stress or emphasis on the note.

- THE DOT

This sign means *less* staccato than the wedge. The key is kept down somewhat longer than when the preceding indication is used.

- DOTS UNDER A SLUR

This means still *less* staccato.

BEETHOVEN'S LEGATO

The modern school of legato playing began with Clementi, whose piano method Beethoven endorsed. Beethoven's pupil, Carl Czerny, said that Beethoven's legato was "controlled to an incomparable degree, which at that time all pianists regarded as impossible of execution, for even after Mozart's time the choppy, short, detached manner of playing was the fashion."

In his piano method, Clementi states that when no indications appear in the composer's music to indicate legato or staccato playing, "the best rule is to adhere chiefly to the legato, reserving the staccato to give spirit occasionally to certain passages, and to set off the higher beauties of the legato."

The editorial suggestions in light gray print will solve most performance problems for students who are uncertain as to how certain appoggiaturas should be played, or whether to play legato or detached, etc.